Discovering Re

Buddhism

FOUNDATION EDITION

SUE PENNEY

Heinemann

Heinemann Educational Publishers
Halley Court, Jordan Hill, Oxford OX2 8EJ
a division of Reed Educational & Professional Publishing Ltd

OXFORD MELBOURNE AUCKLAND
JOHANNESBURG BLANTYRE GABORONE
IBADAN PORTSMOUTH NH (US) CHICAGO

Heinemann is a registered trademark of Reed Educational & Professional Publishing Ltd

03 02 01 00
10 9 8 7 6 5 4 3

British Library Cataloguing in Publication Data

ISBN 0 435 304763

Designed and typeset by Visual Image
Illustrated by Visual Image
Cover design by Keith Shaw at Threefold Design
Printed and bound in Great Britain by Bath Colourbooks, Glasgow

Acknowledgements

The publishers would like to thank the following for permission to use photographs:
Andes Press Agency p. 42; Aspect Picture Library p. 37; Christine Bluntzer/Impact Photos
p. 20; The Bridgeman Art Library pp. 28, 29; The J Allan Cash Photo Library pp. 13, 22,
25, 33; Circa Photo Library pp. 19, 43; Bruce Coleman Ltd p. 6; Douglas Dickens pp. 10,
30; C M Dixon p. 23; Anil Goonewardene p. 27; Sally and Richard Greenhill p. 47; Robert
Harding Picture Library pp. 31, 32, 35; Graham Harrison pp. 17, 18, 40; The Hutchinson
Library pp. 26, 46; Barry Lewis/Network p. 11; G Mermet/Impact Photos p. 44; Christine
Osborne Pictures p. 45; Pana/Press Association p. 36; Ann and Bury Peerless pp. 8, 9, 38;
Still Pictures p. 14; Topham Picturepoint p. 21; Zefa Pictures pp. 24, 34.

The publishers would like to thank the Hutchison Library for permission to reproduce the
cover photograph.

The publishers have made every effort to trace copyright holders. However, if any material
has been incorrectly acknowledged we would be pleased to correct this at the earliest
opportunity.

Contents

MAP: where the main religions began

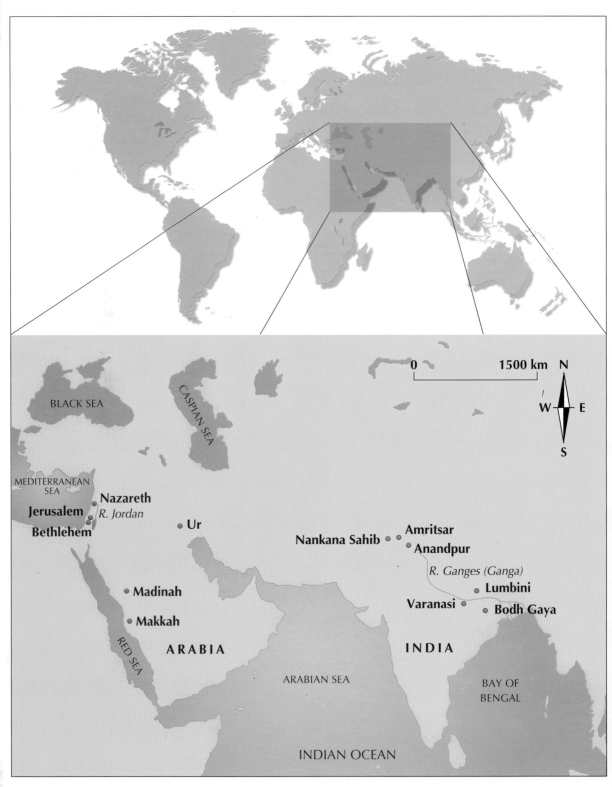

BLACK SEA

CASPIAN SEA

MEDITERRANEAN SEA

0   1500 km   N

W   E

S

Nazareth

Jerusalem *R. Jordan*

Bethlehem

• Ur

Nankana Sahib • • **Amritsar**

• **Anandpur**

R. Ganges (Ganga)

• **Madinah**

• **Lumbini**

Varanasi • • **Bodh Gaya**

• **Makkah**

RED SEA

ARABIA

INDIA

ARABIAN SEA

BAY OF BENGAL

INDIAN OCEAN

TIMECHART: when the main religions began

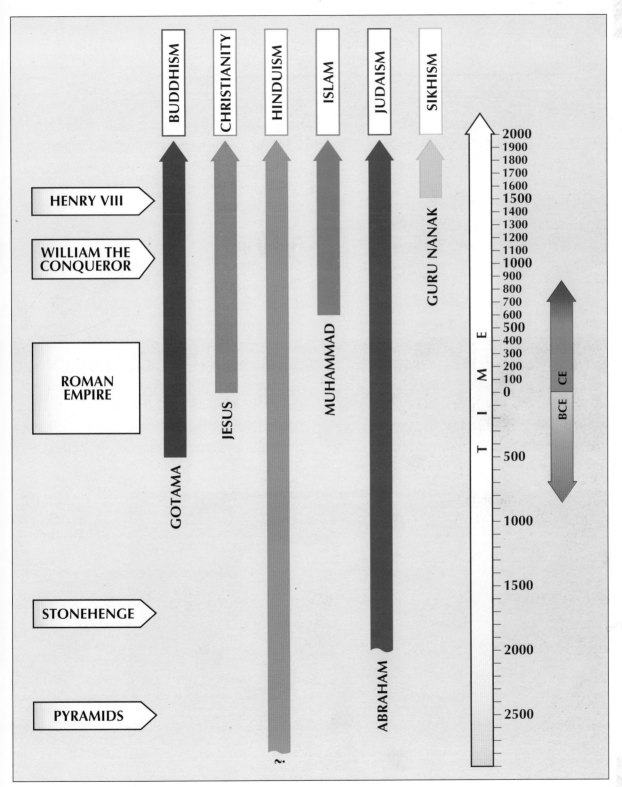

Note about dating systems   In this book dates are not called BC and AD which is the Christian dating system. The letters BCE and CE are used instead. BCE stands for 'Before the Common Era' and CE stands for 'Common Era'. BCE and CE can be used by people of all religions, Christians too. The year numbers are not changed.

Introducing Buddhism

This section tells you something about who Buddhists are.

The teaching we call Buddhism began in India about 2500 years ago. Today, there are estimated to be about 327 million Buddhists in the world.

What do Buddhists believe?

Buddhists follow the teachings of Siddattha Gotama. He lived in India in the sixth century BCE. Siddattha Gotama is called the **Buddha**. This was not his name. It is a special title. It means someone who has gained **Enlightenment**. Enlightenment means being able to see things as they really are. (Think of turning on a light so you can see better.) Buddhists believe that the Buddha saw the truth about what the world is like. He found the answer to why nothing in the world is perfect. They believe that by following the teachings of the Buddha, other people can gain Enlightenment, too.

Buddhists do not believe in a God who is all-powerful. They do not believe that the Buddha was anything more than a human being. They believe he was important because he gained Enlightenment, and chose to teach other people how to gain it.

Rebirth

Buddhists believe that unless someone gains Enlightenment, when they die they will be reborn. They believe that being born, growing old, dying and being reborn is a cycle which goes on and on. Buddhists aim to achieve Enlightenment so that they can break out of this cycle. Breaking out of the cycle is called **Nirvana** (sometimes spelled **Nibbana**). Nirvana is perfect peace, the end of everything that is not perfect (see page 11).

A lotus flower

Buddhists try to reach Nirvana by following the Buddha's teaching and by **meditation**. Meditation means training your mind so that you can really concentrate. It is explained in more detail on page 22.

A wheel is the symbol of Buddhism

Symbols of Buddhism

The **symbol** most often used for Buddhism is a wheel with eight spokes. They remind Buddhists that the Buddha taught about eight ways of living (see page 16).

Another symbol is the **lotus** flower. It grows in mud at the bottom of a pond, but produces a beautiful flower. Buddhists say that this is a symbol of rising above all the things which are not satisfactory in life, and gaining Enlightenment.

Test yourself

Who was the Buddha?

What does Buddha mean?

What is Nirvana?

What is meditation?

What symbol is used for Buddhism?

Think it through

1 What does Enlightenment mean? What do Buddhists believe the Buddha discovered when he gained Enlightenment?

2 How do Buddhists believe they can gain Nirvana?

3 Use the picture opposite to help you draw a picture of a lotus flower. What is it a symbol of? Explain why Buddhists believe it is a useful symbol.

The life of the Buddha

This section tells you about the life of Siddattha Gotama, the Buddha.

Siddattha's early life

Siddattha Gotama was an Indian prince. He was born at Lumbini, in the country we now call Nepal. The stories say that when he was born, wise men said that he would be great. But they said that if he ever saw anyone who was very unhappy, he would become the leader of a religion, not the leader of a country. Siddattha's father wanted his son to be a great ruler, so he ordered that no sick or old people should be allowed to come near the palace. Siddattha was not allowed to leave the palace grounds. He grew up, married a beautiful girl and they had a son. It seemed that he had everything he could want.

Siddattha discovers suffering

However, Siddattha became bored with his sheltered life in the palace. One day, he disobeyed his father's orders to stay in the palace grounds. He went out riding. While he was out, he saw four things that he found very disturbing. He saw an old man, and a sick man. Then he saw a funeral, with people weeping. He had never seen anything like this before. Then he saw a holy man, who had given up his home, his family and everything he owned. The holy man spent his life trying to find the answers to the problem of suffering in the world. He was contented and happy.

Siddattha decided that he must try to find the answers to this problem, too. That night he left the palace. He took off his royal robes, shaved his head, and put on the simple clothes of a holy man.

Siddattha's search for Enlightenment

Siddattha's search for Enlightenment lasted for six years. He tried many different ways. He spent time with great teachers. He spent years living with a group of **monks** who ate and drank almost nothing. He found that

This old painting shows Siddattha meeting suffering

The Mahabodhi Temple at Bodh Gaya

New words

Bodhi tree the 'tree of wisdom' under which the Buddha gained Enlightenment
Cremate to burn a body after death
Monks men who dedicate their life to religion
Stupas Buddhist holy places

starving himself did not help, so he began eating and drinking again. The monks left him in disgust. Siddattha travelled on.

One day, Siddattha sat down under a great tree and meditated. Today, this tree is called the **bodhi tree**, which means 'tree of wisdom'. The place is called Bodh Gaya. Siddattha meditated for a day and a night, and gained Enlightenment there. He understood why suffering happens and how it can be stopped.

The Buddha

From this time on, Siddattha was called the Buddha. Buddhist teaching says that when Siddattha had gained Enlightenment he could have left earthly life behind. Instead he chose to stay and spend the rest of his life teaching. He passed away at the age of 80 (Buddhists do not say he died). His body was **cremated**. The ashes were buried in special buildings called **stupas**.

Test yourself

Where was Siddattha born?

What is a monk?

What does 'bodhi tree' mean?

What is cremation?

What is a stupa?

Think it through

1 What were the four things which Siddattha saw when he went riding? Why do you think he found them so disturbing?

2 The monks were trying to gain Enlightenment, too. Why were they so disgusted when Siddattha began eating and drinking again?

3 Draw four pictures to show important events in the life of the Buddha. Use these titles: Prince, Meeting suffering, Meditating, Teaching.

Buddhist teachings

This section outlines important Buddhist teachings.

The Three Jewels
The Three Jewels sum up the most important Buddhist beliefs.

> I take refuge in the Buddha
> I take refuge in the **Dhamma**
> I take refuge in the **Sangha**

A jewel is something that is beautiful and very precious. Buddhists feel that these three teachings are like jewels. A refuge is somewhere which is very safe. Saying that they take refuge in these teachings is another way of showing how important Buddhists think the teachings are. Buddhists repeat them every day.

The first jewel
The first jewel is the Buddha. Buddhists respect him because he showed the way to Enlightenment. Enlightenment is not the same as just knowing things. It means finding them out for yourself, and realizing they are true. (Think of learning to ride a bicycle. You can be told what to do, and know in your head what to do, but you still have to discover for yourself how to do it.) Buddhists believe that they must gain Enlightenment before they can stop being reborn, and enter Nirvana.

The second jewel
The second jewel is the Buddha's teaching, which is called the Dhamma. The word dhamma means 'natural law'. In other words, Buddhists believe that these teachings have always been there, and have always been true. They do not believe that the Buddha thought them up. They believe he was important because he explained the teachings so that people could understand them.

The third jewel
The third jewel is the Sangha. This means everyone who follows the Buddha, especially Buddhist monks and **nuns**.

A Buddhist temple in Myanmar (Burma)

Buddhists at a temple in Scotland

Monks and nuns are men and women who have chosen to make their religion the most important thing in their lives. They are very important in Buddhism. They offer help to other Buddhists as they try to follow the Buddha's teachings.

Nirvana

Nirvana means 'going out' – like a fire goes out when it has no fuel. Buddhists say that it is not possible to describe Nirvana. You can only say what it is not. It is not life or death. It is being free of greed and anger, and the end of everything that is not perfect. It is when 'you' does not exist any longer. Buddhists believe that it is the only way to be totally free.

New words

Dhamma the Buddha's teachings
Nuns women who dedicate their life to religion
Sangha followers of the Buddha, especially monks and nuns

Test yourself

What is a refuge?

What is the Dhamma?

What does Sangha mean?

What is a nun?

What does Nirvana mean?

Think it through

1 What reasons can you think of why Buddhists call these teachings jewels?

2 Explain what Buddhists believe the Dhamma is. Why do they believe that what the Buddha did is important?

3 Buddhists say that you can only describe Nirvana by saying what it is not. What other things can you think of which are important but difficult to explain? (**Clue**: hope? fear? love?)

Teachings of the Buddha I

This section tells you about part of the Buddha's teachings.

After the Buddha's Enlightenment, he spent nearly 50 years teaching. Buddhists believe that his teachings tell them how to live. When people describe the Buddha's teachings, they usually divide them into three main parts. The first part is the Three Signs of Being.

The Three Signs of Being

The Three Signs of Being are **dukkha**, **anicca** and **anatta**. These are three of the most important words in Buddhist belief.

Dukkha

Dukkha is often translated as 'suffering', but it means much more than pain. It includes things like being bored or uncomfortable. It means anything that is not satisfactory. Buddhists believe that life is dukkha, because nothing in life is completely perfect. The Buddha said that dukkha is everywhere, and no one can escape it. His teaching was a way of rising above it.

Anicca

Anicca is a way of saying that nothing lasts. Everything that we know is changing. This is easy to understand when you think about plants or animals or even people. Even things that seem to be there forever, like mountains, do change very slowly. The Buddha said that there is no rest except Nirvana.

Anatta

Anatta means 'no-**soul**'. Many religions teach that there is a soul or spirit which never dies. The Buddha said that there is no such thing. He said that people are made up of five parts – body, feelings, thoughts, ideas, and awareness of things around them. Every person is made up of these five things. This teaching is connected to the Buddhist teaching about rebirth.

Rebirth

Buddhists believe in rebirth, but they do not believe there is a soul which goes from one body to another to be reborn. They believe that what carries on to the next life is a 'life-force' which the person has made in this life. Good things that a person does will lead to a 'higher' life next time. Bad things which a person does will lead to a 'lower' life next time. All past lives have an effect.

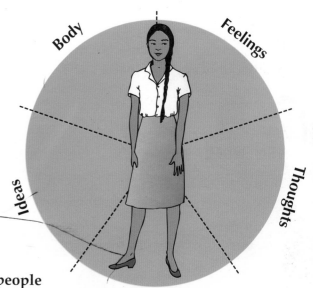

The Buddha taught that people are made up of five parts

Buddhists worshipping at a temple in Thailand

If you find this hard to understand, think of a row of dominoes standing on end. If you push the first one, you make a force which will make all the rest fall over without you doing anything else.

Buddhists believe that the only way to break out of this 'life-force' is to reach Nirvana. They believe they can do this by following the Buddha's teachings, and by meditating.

New words

Anatta belief that there is nothing called a soul
Anicca belief that nothing lasts
Dukkha belief that nothing is satisfactory
Soul a spirit which goes on living after a person's death

Test yourself

What does dukkha mean?

What does anicca mean?

What does anatta mean?

What is a soul?

How many parts did the Buddha say people are made of?

Think it through

1 Explain why Buddhists believe that life is dukkha. Why is this such an important part of Buddhist belief?

2 What did the Buddha teach about what makes a person? What do you think about the teaching?

3 Explain what Buddhists believe about how actions in this life affect future lives. What difference do you think it would make to the world if everyone believed this?

Teachings of the Buddha II

This section tells you about the Four Noble Truths.

The Four Noble Truths

The Four Noble Truths were the main part of the first teaching the Buddha gave after he had gained Enlightenment. He taught about the reasons why everything in the world is dukkha (not satisfactory), and what people can do to rise above it. He said that when people realized the Four Noble Truths, they would be able to change their lives.

Dukkha is boredom and discomfort as well as suffering

The First Noble Truth

Dukkha happens everywhere all the time.

The Buddha said that everything in the world is dukkha. This is because nothing can ever be exactly as we wish it to be. Every person's life includes the effect from the lives they have lived before, so no one's life can ever be perfect. They will only be able to rise above this when they reach Nirvana.

The Second Noble Truth

Dukkha is caused by being greedy and selfish.

Everybody always thinks more about themselves than they do about other people. We always want the best for ourselves. We would rather do what we want than what other people want. (Think of your playground at break!) This selfishness is the cause of dukkha in the world. The Buddha said that even being reborn is selfish, and people should try to break out of the rebirth cycle.

The Third Noble Truth

Greed and selfishness can be stopped.

When you no longer want anything for yourself you can leave dukkha behind. You

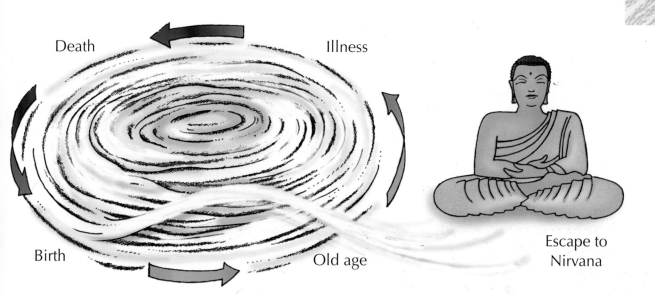

Death

Illness

Birth

Old age

Escape to
Nirvana

The circle of rebirth

can see beyond yourself, and believe that
you are no longer important. A Buddhist
believes that this can only happen when
you have broken out of the circle of rebirth,
and reached perfect freedom. This freedom
is Nirvana.

The Fourth Noble Truth

The way to stop selfishness is to follow
the Noble Eightfold Path.

The Noble Eightfold Path is the way the
Buddha taught that people should live. It is
sometimes called the Middle Way. The
Buddha said that people live as if they are
trying to walk through muddy ground.
They can only be helped by people who are
standing on firm ground. The Noble
Eightfold Path is the way to find this firm
ground. It is explained in the next section.

Test yourself

How many Noble Truths are there?

When did the Buddha first teach
about the Noble Truths?

How can you rise above dukkha?

How can selfishness be stopped?

Think it through

1 Explain in your own words what the
Four Noble Truths teach. Why are
they so important for Buddhists?

2 What did the Buddha say about
being selfish? How would you
explain what being selfish means?

3 The Buddha taught that selfishness
leads to suffering. Write a short
story or draw a cartoon strip to
show that this is true.

15

Teachings of the Buddha III

This section tells you about the part of the Buddha's teaching called the Noble Eightfold Path.

The Middle Way

The Buddha said that you should not have too much or too little of anything. A life of luxury with too much to eat and drink is no better than a life where you starve yourself and punish your body. He said that the 'Middle Way' to Nirvana is between these two extremes. It is called the Noble Eightfold Path.

The Noble Eightfold Path

The Noble Eightfold Path shows eight ways that people should live. You need to follow all these ways. There is no point just choosing to follow some of them. Each way begins with the word right. This does not just mean 'right' like a sum is right or wrong. It means 'best possible', too.

Right viewpoint

Right viewpoint means looking at life in the right way. You will not be able to reach Nirvana unless you do this. You need to accept that the Buddha's teachings are true.

Right thought

Your mind is very powerful, so it must be used in the right way. Thinking about other people in the right way will mean that you are not selfish.

Right speech

You should make sure that your words are always kind and helpful. You should not tell lies, swear or gossip about other people.

Right action

The way you behave is important. You should not kill or steal, and you should treat

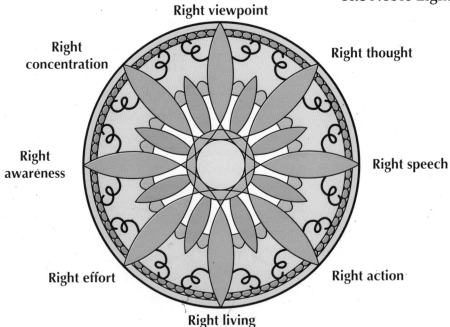

The Noble Eightfold Path

Right viewpoint

Right concentration

Right thought

Right awareness

Right speech

Right effort

Right action

Right living

Lighting candles is part of Buddhist worship

other people well. You should be faithful to your husband or wife. You should not do anything which harms your body. This includes things like smoking or taking drugs.

Right living

The job you do is important, and you should work to the best of your ability. You should not have a job which harms others, or means you need to kill things.

Right effort

You must work hard to do good, as well as train yourself to avoid bad things.

Right awareness

You need to control your mind so that you see things around you in the right way.

Right concentration

You can train your mind to concentrate by meditation. This means you can become a calm and peaceful person. It will help you to understand things better.

Test yourself

What did the Buddha mean by the 'Middle Way'?

What does the Noble Eightfold Path show?

What does 'right' mean in this path?

Why are right thoughts about other people so important?

How do Buddhists believe they can control their minds?

Think it through

1 What do you think about the Middle Way as a way to live? Give reasons for your answer.

2 What sort of jobs do you think a Buddhist would need to avoid if they are to work without harming others?

3 Do you think it would be easy for you to follow the Noble Eightfold Path? Make a list of the things about yourself you would have to change.

Theravada and Mahayana

This section tells you about the two main groups of Buddhists.

All Buddhists follow the teachings of the Buddha. Not all of them think in exactly the same way about the teachings and the way that things should be done. This means that there are different groups of Buddhists. In Buddhism, the groups are called 'schools'. There are two main schools in Buddhism. These are called **Theravada** Buddhism and **Mahayana** Buddhism.

Theravada Buddhists

Theravada means 'teachings of the elders'. An elder is a respected leader of a religion. Theravada Buddhism is sometimes called southern Buddhism, because most of its followers live in countries like Sri Lanka, Myanmar (Burma) and Thailand.

Theravada Buddhism teaches that every person must gain Enlightenment for themselves. The Buddha showed people the way in his teachings and Buddhists follow him as a guide. Theravada Buddhists do not pray to the Buddha, because they believe that he was only a man. His teachings, not the Buddha himself, help people to gain Enlightenment.

Monks and nuns do not have to think about a job or a family, so many Theravada Buddhists think that this is the best way to live. They believe that nuns and monks are closer to Nirvana than other people.

Mahayana Buddhism

Mahayana means 'great vehicle'. This is a way of saying that there is room for different ways of reaching Nirvana. Mahayana and Theravada Buddhism have many of the same ideas. In some cases, Mahayana Buddhism has changed the way these ideas are explained. For example, they believe there have been many Buddhas and **Bodhisattvas**, who can help them in their lives. A Bodhisattva is someone who has gained Enlightenment, but has chosen to be reborn so that they can help others to achieve it, too.

Theravada Buddhist monks in Myanmar

18

Buddhism

A statue of a Bodhisattva

There are many thousands of Bodhisattvas. Mahayana Buddhists pray to them for help in achieving Enlightenment and for help with problems in everyday life. They meditate to try to become more like them.

Mahayana Buddhism is most popular in the countries of Japan, Korea and Tibet. This is why it is sometimes called northern Buddhism.

Test yourself

What does Theravada mean?

Where is Theravada Buddhism most popular?

What does Mahayana mean?

Where is Mahayana Buddhism most popular?

What is the other name for Mahayana Buddhism?

Think it through

1 Why do you think the differences between Theravada and Mahayana Buddhism came about?

2 Why do you think Theravada Buddhists believe that a monk or nun is closer to Nirvana than an ordinary person?

3 What is a Bodhisattva? Why do you think many Buddhists pray to Bodhisattvas?

New words

Bodhisattva person who has gained Enlightenment, but has chosen to be reborn to be able to help others

Mahayana 'great vehicle' – school of Buddhism

Theravada 'teachings of the elders' – school of Buddhism

Other schools of Buddhism

This section tells you about three of the schools of Mahayana Buddhism.

Zen Buddhism

Zen is a Japanese word which means meditation. Zen Buddhism is most popular in Japan and Korea, and in China, where it is called Cha'an. Zen Buddhists believe that meditation is very important, and they meditate for many hours each day.

Zen Buddhists aim to silence thoughts which are unhelpful. They call this 'training the mind'. They try to cause their mind to leave its usual ways of thought to 'shock' it into understanding. They believe that this will eventually lead to Enlightenment, which they say comes as a flash of higher understanding. Zen Buddhist monks live in **monasteries**, and their training is usually very strict.

Pure Land Buddhism

Many followers of Pure Land Buddhism live in Japan. Pure Land Buddhists pray to the Buddha Amida, who is Lord of the Pure Land. After life in this world, the Pure Land is a place without suffering where it is easier to achieve Nirvana.

Pure Land Buddhists believe that Amida will help them to get to the Pure Land. They often use a special prayer to Amida. This is 'Nembutsu Amida', which means 'I call on you, Amida'. Prayers which are repeated over and over again like this are called **mantras**. Buddhists believe that mantras have special power.

The ideas of Pure Land Buddhism are not accepted by many other Buddhists, who feel that they do not follow the teachings of the Buddha Gotama.

A Zen monastery garden

Tibetan Buddhism

Tibetan Buddhists believe that a monk called the Dalai Lama is special. They believe he is an appearance of the Bodhisattva who is most special for the country of Tibet.

When the Dalai Lama dies, a careful search is made for the monk who is the next appearance of the Bodhisattva. Mantras and prayers to this Bodhisattva are written on prayer wheels and prayer flags. A prayer wheel is a cylinder with paper rolled up inside it. As the wheels are turned and the flags blow in the wind, Tibetan Buddhists believe that the prayers are repeated over and over again. Making prayers which are repeated like this is a way of getting **merit**. Merit is the reward for doing good things. It helps you on your way to Nirvana.

New words

Mantras sacred chants which Buddhists believe have special power
Merit reward for doing good things
Monasteries places where monks live

Test yourself

What does Zen mean?

What is a monastery?

Who is the Buddha Amida?

What is a mantra?

Why do Tibetan Buddhists believe that the Dalai Lama is special?

Think it through

1 Look at the photo opposite of the Zen monastery garden. Write a few sentences describing it. How do you think it would make you feel if you were sitting in it?

2 Write a couple of sentences about what Pure Land Buddhists believe. Why do some Buddhists not agree with these teachings?

3 Explain what prayer wheels and prayer flags are. Why do you think Tibetan Buddhists use them?

Prayer wheels and prayer flags at a temple in Nepal

Worship I

This section tells you about how Buddhists worship.

Some Buddhists do not like using the word worship, because it usually means praying to a God or gods. Worship in this book means the way Buddhists meditate and read the holy books.

There is no special day of the week when Buddhists worship. Days before the moon is new, full or at half-moon are important. Full moon days are most important of all. This is because the Buddha is said to have been born, enlightened and to have passed away at times when the moon was full.

Meditation

Meditation

Most Buddhists think that meditation is the most important part of worship. They usually sit on the floor, with crossed legs. They try to empty their mind of all thoughts. This means that they can concentrate on things that are really important. The point of meditation is to 'rise above' the world and its problems, and any worries you may have. Buddhists believe that meditating helps them to become better people, and will help them to achieve Enlightenment.

Group worship

Buddhists usually meet for worship in a special building called a temple. There is usually a room which contains a **shrine**. This is beautifully decorated with gold and lots of coloured patterns. It contains an **image** of the Buddha, called a **Buddharupa**.

There are no seats in a shrine room. Worshippers sit cross-legged on the floor. They greet the Buddharupa by bowing or putting their hands together. Sometimes they lie flat on the floor. These are ways of showing how much they respect the image.

People often offer gifts of flowers and **incense**, which is a sweet smelling perfume, and light candles or small lamps. Monks often read from the holy books, and a senior monk may give a talk.

After the worship ceremony, people often stay and drink tea together. This can be part of worship, too. The people sit quietly, drinking specially prepared tea from beautiful crockery. There are often flower arrangements. The idea is to be surrounded by peace and beauty.

Individual worship

Buddhists who are worshipping on their own usually meditate and read from the holy books. They may burn incense and offer small presents to the Buddharupa. Flowers and grains of rice are the usual sort of offerings.

Worship usually includes lighting candles. Buddhists believe that the light from the candles is a symbol. It shows how the Buddha's teaching can help you to see the important things in life. Theravada Buddhists do not pray to the Buddha, but Mahayana Buddhists pray to Bodhisattvas as part of their worship.

A Buddharupa (notice the small gifts which have been offered)

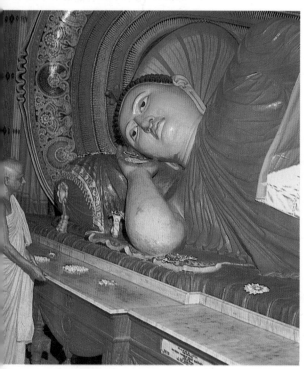

New words

Buddharupa image of the Buddha
Image statue
Incense sweet smelling perfume
Shrine special place for worship

Test yourself

What is a shrine?

What is an image?

What is the image of the Buddha called?

What is incense?

Why do Buddhists light candles?

Think it through

1 Make a list of ways in which Buddhists show respect to the Buddharupa. How many ways can you think of in which people can show respect to others in everyday life?

2 Explain what a tea-drinking ceremony is like. Explain how ceremonies like this can be part of Buddhist worship.

3 Working in small groups, discuss how meditation might help you to become a better person. Present your conclusions to the other groups.

Worship II

This section tells you about the places where Buddhists worship.

Shrines

A shrine is a place which is special to people who follow a particular religion. A Buddhist shrine contains an image of the Buddha, called a Buddharupa. A Buddhist shrine usually contains holders for flowers and candles, too.

Different Buddhist schools have quite different shrines. For example, Zen Buddhist shrines are usually very plain and simple. Other schools have shrines which may be highly decorated. Buddhists usually worship in front of shrines, either in a temple or at home.

Monasteries

In countries where most people are Buddhists, there are many monasteries. Ordinary people often go there to worship and study. Many children go to the local monastery to be taught to read and write by the monks. Many monasteries are like a small village, with lots of buildings and huts where the monks live (see pages 40–41). The most important room in a monastery is the shrine room. This is used for worship, and also for meetings of the monks.

The monastery gardens

An important part of a Buddhist monastery is the garden. Many monasteries have a well-planned garden, planted with trees and shrubs. The gardens are places of peace and quiet. The plants are symbols of the Buddha's teaching that nothing lasts. They grow, die and their seeds grow again. In countries where they will grow, monastery gardens often include a bodhi tree. This is the kind of tree which the Buddha was sitting under when he gained Enlightenment. Buddhists believe that these trees are very important.

Stupas

Many Buddhists go to worship at important stupas. A stupa is a sort of building, shaped

A Japanese Buddhist woman worshipping at the shrine in her house

The stupa at Bodnath, in Nepal (the eyes are symbols that the Buddha sees everything)

like a small round hill. After the Buddha had passed away his body was cremated, and the ashes were taken to eight different places which had been important in his life. Stupas were built where the ashes were buried. Another two were built – one over the place where his body had been burned, and one where the container which had held the ashes was buried. This made ten stupas which contained remains of the Buddha.

Later, other stupas were built to remember Buddhists who were special because they were teachers or holy people. Some stupas now have a monastery built around them.

Test yourself

What does a shrine contain?

Where do Buddhists worship?

Why do Buddhists believe that the bodhi tree is important?

What is a stupa?

How many stupas contain remains of the Buddha?

Think it through

1 Think of as many reasons as you can why the shrine room is the most important room in a monastery.

2 What do plants in a monastery garden symbolize? Why might a place of peace and quiet be important to Buddhists?

3 Explain why the first Buddhist stupas were built. Why do you think Buddhists might want to go and visit them?

Holy books

This section tells you about the holy books of Buddhism.

After the Buddha

When the Buddha was teaching, people remembered what he said. Many people in those days could not read or write. Even very important things were not often written down. When the Buddha passed away, a special meeting was arranged for 500 Buddhist monks. Two of the Buddha's closest friends recited all the Buddha's teachings. All the monks repeated it together, and they all agreed that it was correct.

The Buddhist canons

For about 400 years, all the teaching was passed down by the monks. There were meetings to check that everything was still being remembered correctly. Then people began to think that the teaching should be written down.

There are two main collections of teaching. A collection of teaching is called a **canon**. The two canons have the names of the languages in which they were first written. One is called the **Pali** Canon. The other is called the **Sanskrit** Canon.

The Pali Canon was written down first. It is also called the **Tipitaka**. The two collections are different. The Pali Canon is used by Theravada Buddhists. The Sanskrit Canon is used by Mahayana Buddhists. The fact that the books were written down in two languages is the reason why important Buddhist words are sometimes spelled in two different ways.

The Tipitaka

Tipitaka means 'three baskets'. It is probably called this because it was first written on palm leaves which were kept in baskets. The first basket contains the rules which monks should follow, and some stories. The second basket contains the teachings of the Buddha. The third basket contains writings which help to explain the Buddha's teachings.

The most important of these three baskets is the second one. This contains the Buddha's teachings. It is called the **Sutta** Pitaka. A sutta (or **sutra** in Sanskrit) is a small piece of teaching. The most important part is the Path of Teaching. This contains the teaching about the Four Noble Truths and the Noble Eightfold Path (see pages 14–17).

Boys reading from the holy books

Buddhist nuns in Britain studying the holy books

Mahayana Buddhist teachings

Mahayana Buddhists also follow the teachings of the Tipitaka, but they disagree about which teachings are the most important. Mahayana Buddhists believe that two of the most important teachings are the Diamond Sutra and the Lotus Sutra. Mahayana Buddhists do not believe that the Pali Canon contains all of the Buddha's teachings. They believe the Sanskrit Canon contains other teachings of the Buddha.

New words

Canon collection of writings (the Buddha's teachings)

Sanskrit very old Indian language

Sutta (Sutra) small part of a teaching

Tipitaka 'three baskets' (collection of Buddhist teachings)

Pali ancient language, said to have been spoken by the Buddha

Test yourself

In what two languages were the teachings first written down?

What does Tipitaka mean?

What is a sutta?

What are the most important teachings for Mahayana Buddhists?

Think it through

1 Why was the Tipitaka probably given this name? What does it contain?

2 Why do you think Mahayana Buddhists gave the names Diamond and Lotus to teachings they believed were important?

3 Collect as much information as you can about Buddhist teachings. Work in groups to make a wall display about what you have found.

Symbols in Buddhism

This section tells you about some of the symbols which Buddhists use.

A symbol is a way of showing something without using words. Using a symbol means that complicated things can be made clear without needing a long explanation. Buddhism uses many different symbols.

Flowers

The lotus flower is often used as a symbol for Buddhism. (This was explained on page 6.) Flowers are often used as a symbol of the Buddhist belief that everything is dukkha (not satisfactory), too. They are pretty and they smell nice, but they soon die. Even though they are beautiful, they show that everything in life is not perfect.

Candles

Candles are used as a symbol of the Buddha's teaching. Just as a candle brings light to a dark room, so Buddhists believe that what the Buddha taught can show them the way to live.

Images of the Buddha

Images of the Buddha include lots of symbols. He is usually shown standing, sitting or lying down. If he is standing, he usually has one hand raised, to show that he is blessing people. If he is shown sitting down, he is usually meditating. His right

hand is often touching the ground. This comes from a story about his Enlightenment, and is a symbol that he is calling on the Earth to take notice of his teachings. Pictures and images of him lying down usually show him just before he passed away.

Buddhists use up to 32 symbols to show that the Buddha was a special person. For example, he is often shown with a 'dome' on the top of this head. This shows that he had special talents. He is often shown with

Images of the Buddha often show special symbols

A mandala

man. His long ears show that he came from an important family, and also that he could hear things that other people could not.

Mandalas

Mandalas are especially important in Tibetan Buddhism. They are complicated patterns usually made with coloured sand. Mandala means circle, and mandalas are made up of circles, triangles, squares and diamonds.

The Wheel of the Law (the wheel with eight spokes which is used as a symbol of Buddhism) is a mandala. Sometimes mandalas include pictures of the Buddha or a Bodhisattva as well. Many Buddhists use mandalas to help them meditate.

a mark on his forehead, which is called the third eye. No one really thinks that the Buddha had this, but it is a way of showing that he could see things ordinary people cannot see. He is shown with curled hair, which is a symbol that he was a very holy

New word

Mandalas specially designed patterns

Test yourself

What are flowers a symbol of for Buddhists?

What are candles a symbol of for Buddhists?

How many symbols can be used in images of the Buddha?

What is a mandala?

What is the Wheel of the Law?

Think it through

1 What is a symbol? Why do you think many religions use symbols as part of their teaching?

2 Explain why flowers and candles are good symbols for Buddhists to use.

3 What symbols can you see on the picture of the Buddharupa opposite? Explain what the symbols are and why they are used.

Pilgrimage

This section tells you about some of the important places which Buddhists visit.

A **pilgrimage** is a journey which people make because of their religion. Buddhists may go to places where the Buddha lived or taught. They believe that this will help them in their own search for Enlightenment.

Lumbini

The Buddha was born at a place called Lumbini. This is now in the country called Nepal. It is quite a difficult place to get to. A small community of monks live there and there are temples where people can meditate. The place where the Buddha was born has a simple stone pillar which says on it 'Here the Buddha was born'.

Bodh Gaya

Bodh Gaya is the place where the Buddha gained Enlightenment. Buddhists go there from all over the world. It is one of the most important places of pilgrimage. A bodhi tree grows there. It is supposed to have grown from a seed of the same tree that the Buddha sat under when he was meditating. Pilgrims walk around this tree, and sit under it to meditate. They have bare feet and heads as a sign of respect. There are temples nearby. (There is a picture of the main temple at Bodh Gaya on page 9.)

Stupas

Many Buddhists visit the stupas where part of the Buddha's ashes are buried. When a

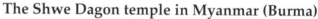

The Shwe Dagon temple in Myanmar (Burma)

Sunrise at
Sri Pada

Buddhist visits a stupa, he or she walks around it three times. This remembers the Three Jewels which are the most important part of Buddhist teaching. Temples are often built at a stupa.

Some temples contain remains of the Buddha, too. For example, the Shwe Dagon Temple in Myanmar has eight of the Buddha's hairs. In Sri Lanka, there is a festival every year in the town of Kandy. Kandy has a temple where one of the Buddha's teeth is kept (see page 34).

Sri Pada

Sri Pada is a mountain in Sri Lanka. It is very important for Buddhists because they believe that the Buddha visited it. At the top of the mountain is a stone which has marks like footprints on it. Buddhists believe that these were made by the Buddha.

New word

Pilgrimage journey made for religious reasons

Test yourself

What is a pilgrimage?

What happened at Lumbini?

Why does a Buddhist walk around a stupa three times?

Where is Sri Pada?

Think it through

1 Why do you think many Buddhists go on pilgrimage to Bodh Gaya?

2 What reasons can you give for why stupas are especially important for Buddhists to visit?

3 Imagine you are a Buddhist on a pilgrimage. Write a postcard to friends at home, telling them what you have been doing. Then use one of the pictures in this book to help you draw a picture for your postcard.

Festivals I

This section tells you about festivals in Thailand, a Theravada Buddhist country.

Songkran

Songkran takes place in April. It lasts for three days, and includes the Thai New Year. People go to the monasteries and give presents like food and flowers to the monks. New Year is a chance to make a new start, so everyone wears new or clean clothes.

Water is very important in the festival of Songkran. There are often water fights on the streets, and boat races are held on the rivers. People may also release fish which they have cared for during the dry season when the rivers had little water. Sometimes caged birds are released instead. This follows the Buddha's teaching about being kind to all living things.

Wesak

The festival of Wesak gets its name from the month in which it is celebrated (May or June in the western calendar). The festival remembers the Buddha's birth, his Enlightenment and his passing away.

Theravada Buddhists believe that these three things all happened on the day when the moon was full in the month of Wesak. It is one of the most important Buddhist festivals and is celebrated by Buddhists all over the world. It is called Vaisakha in some countries. In Britain it is sometimes called Buddha Day. Many Buddhists give each other cards and presents to celebrate the festival.

In Thailand, the people visit the monasteries at Wesak. They listen to the monks giving talks about the Buddha's life.

Celebrating Songkran

The shrines in the temples are beautifully decorated. Part of the celebration includes pouring perfumed water over the shrine's Buddharupa. At night, the Buddharupa is taken out of the shrine and put on a platform outside. The people walk around it carrying lamps so that the image is surrounded by light. It reminds people of the 'light' of the Buddha's teaching.

Kathina

Kathina takes place at the end of the rainy season in Thailand (November in the western calendar). People take presents to the monasteries. This is a way of saying 'thank you' to the monks for all the work they do during the year. Monks are not allowed to own anything themselves, so the presents are given to the monastery, not to one particular person. The presents are things like cloth for new robes and paper or books. Buddhists believe that giving at this time of year will earn merit for the giver. Merit is the reward for doing good things which helps you on your way to Nirvana.

Pouring scented water over the Buddharupa

Test yourself

How long does Songkran last?

When is Wesak held?

What other names are used for Wesak?

What is poured over the Buddharupa?

When does Kathina take place?

Think it through

1 Explain why people might want to surround the Buddharupa with light at Wesak.

2 What sort of presents do people give to the monks at Kathina? What reasons can you think of why they do this?

3 Work in groups to put together a project about Buddhism in Thailand. Collect all the information you can, and see if you can find pictures from travel agents' brochures.

Festivals II

This section tells you about festivals in Sri Lanka. Sri Lanka is also a Theravada Buddhist country.

Wesak

Wesak is the most important Buddhist festival in Sri Lanka. It remembers the three most important events in the Buddha's life – his birth, his Enlightenment and his passing away.

In Sri Lanka, people light their houses with lamps and there are plays and dancing to celebrate the festival. Everyone remembers what the Buddha taught about being kind to other people. They make a special effort to be kind to everyone. Some people set up stalls by the side of the road, and offer free food and drink to anyone who is passing.

Poson

Poson is a special festival for Sri Lanka. It is celebrated on the day of the full moon in the month of Poson (May or June in the western calendar). It remembers the time in 250 BCE when Buddhism was brought to Sri Lanka from India. Two **missionaries** came to tell the people about Buddhism. They were the son and daughter of the Emperor Asoka (see page 38). They arrived in the town of Mihintale. Today, special plays are put on in this town to remind people of how important the missionaries were.

Esala Perahera

Esala Perahera takes place in August. The festival is held in the town of Kandy, and lasts for ten days. There is a temple in Kandy which was built specially to keep

Esala Perahera

Dancing is an important part of many festivals

something which Buddhists think is very precious. It is a **relic** of the Buddha – one of his teeth. It is kept in a special container. Every year there is a procession through the town of Kandy in its honour. Over a hundred elephants take part. The most important elephant carries a container which is an exact copy of the one in the temple. The real one is far too precious to be allowed on the streets.

As well as a festival to celebrate the Buddha, Esala Perahera is a time for enjoying yourself. Fairs and dancers on the streets entertain hundreds of people who go to watch the procession.

New words

Missionary someone who travels to tell people about what they believe
Relic object which is old and treasured (usually remains of a holy person)

Test yourself

What do people remember at Wesak?

When did Buddhism arrive in Sri Lanka?

What is a missionary?

What is Esala Perahera?

Think it through

1 Explain why Wesak is the most important Buddhist festival. How is it celebrated in Sri Lanka?

2 What does Poson celebrate? Why do you think the people of Sri Lanka believe this was so important?

3 What happens at Esala Perahera? What reasons can you give why Buddhists believe that relics of the Buddha should be given so much respect?

Festivals III

This section tells you about Buddhist festivals in Japan. Japan is a Mahayana Buddhist country.

New Year

For Japanese Buddhists, the day before New Year is a very important day of the year. This is when the Evening Bells ceremony takes place. At midnight, the bells in every Buddhist temple in Japan are rung 108 times. This is a special number for Buddhists.

Many Buddhists believe that there are 108 'mortal passions' – things that can cause harm in people's lives. They include things like envy, greed and laziness. Many Buddhists believe that each ring of the bell drives out one of these faults. Ringing the bell also gives them time to think about ways in which they can live better lives in the year to come.

Obon

Obon is the most important Buddhist festival in Japan. It takes place in July. It is a time when Buddhists remember people in their family who have died.

Some Buddhists believe that the spirits of people who have died come back to the family home for the three days of the festival. They light lamps to show them the way, and put flowers on the family shrine to make it pretty for the spirits.

Mahayana Buddhists believe that the Buddha can help you in your life, so praying to the Buddha is part of this festival. They also ask for his help on behalf of the people who have died.

One of the stories which Japanese Buddhists remember at Obon is about how the Buddha helped the mother of one of his friends. She was in the land of ghosts, and the Buddha pulled her out. Some stories say

Ringing the bell at a temple in Japan

Looking after graves is an important part of Higan

that he pulled her out with a rope, so tug of war competitions are often held at Obon.

Higan

Higan takes place twice a year, on the days when day and night are the same length. It is a time for remembering friends and relatives who have died. Buddhists go to the **cemeteries** to clean and look after the graves. They decorate them with flowers.

They also hold special ceremonies which they believe can give merit to the people who have died. They believe this can help the people on their way to Nirvana.

New word

Cemetery place where dead bodies are buried

Test yourself

When does the Evening Bells ceremony take place?

How many times are the bells rung?

When does Obon take place?

When does Higan take place?

What is a cemetery?

Think it through

1 Buddhists believe there are 108 faults which can spoil people's lives. Make a list of as many things as you can which you think fit this description.

2 What do you think Buddhists feel about the spirits of dead relatives coming back to the family home at Obon? What would you feel about it?

3 Why do Japanese Buddhists hold ceremonies to pass on merit to people who have died?

The history of Buddhism

This section tells you a little about the history of Buddhism.

Early days

Buddhists believe that there have been other Buddhas, and there will be Buddhas in the future. Siddattha Gotama was the Buddha who began the Buddhist teaching for the time that we live in. After he had reached Enlightenment, he began teaching. A group of people became his followers. They included the Buddha's own son, Rahula. For 45 years, the Buddha travelled

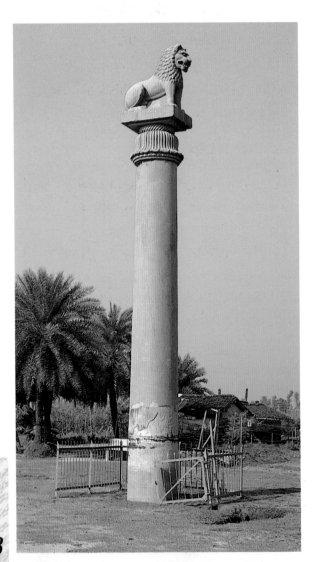

all over India and nearby countries, teaching people about the best way to live.

Emperor Asoka

After the Buddha had passed away, the people who had known him carried on his teaching. More and more people became interested in Buddhism. One of the people who heard about it was the **Emperor** Asoka. He ruled almost the whole of what we call India from 273 BCE to 232 BCE.

Asoka had fought and won many battles. Then he heard the Buddha's teaching about looking after everything that is alive. He started to worry about all the suffering he had caused in the fighting, and **converted** to Buddhism. He tried to rule the country following the teachings of the Buddha. He sent monks and nuns travelling from place to place to tell people about the teachings of Buddhism. His own son and daughter became a monk and a nun, and went to Sri Lanka to tell the people there about Buddhism.

Asoka helped people to learn more about Buddhism. He ordered that stone pillars should be put up at the places where important things had happened to the Buddha. They had writing carved on them explaining why they were there and what had happened at that place. Some of these pillars still survive today.

The spread of Buddhism

As Buddhism spread from one country to another, people did not always agree about

A stone pillar from the time of Asoka

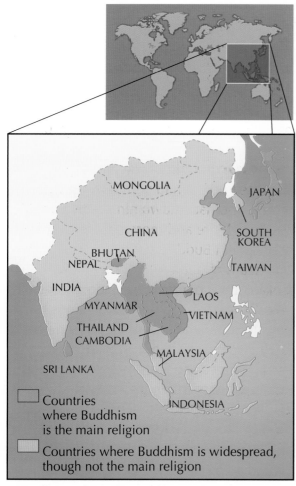

This map shows where most Buddhists live in the world today

the teachings. Some people began to think that one teaching was more important than another. This is why today there are different groups of Buddhists. They all follow the teachings of the Buddha, but they do not all follow them in the same way.

Numbers of Buddhists

It is difficult to guess how many people are Buddhists today, because many Buddhists worship at home, not in temples. Many people believe there are about 327 million Buddhists in the world. Some people think there may be as many as 600 million.

New word

Emperor important ruler of a country
Convert join a religion

Test yourself

What was the Buddha's son called?

How many years did the Buddha preach for?

How long did Asoka rule for?

Why did Asoka order that stone pillars should be put up?

About how many Buddhists are there in the world today?

Think it through

1 Explain why Buddhists believe that the teachings of the Buddha Gotama are important.

2 Why did the Emperor Asoka become a Buddhist? What changes do you think he had to make in his life?

3 If you heard about a religion which was totally new, do you think you would be likely to join it? Would it be easy or difficult?

Buddhist monks and nuns

This section tells you about the way Buddhist monks and nuns live.

Buddhist monks and nuns are men and women who spend their lives meditating and reading the holy books. Nuns and monks live in the same way, although they may follow slightly different rules. This section concentrates on monks, because there are many more monks than nuns.

Who can become a monk?

Any Buddhist man can become a monk. Buddhists do not expect a monk to stay in a monastery all his life. Especially in Theravada Buddhist countries, boys often become monks for a few years. Being in the monastery is like being at school. When they grow up, they leave and find other jobs. Many adults join the monastery for a few months or years. This is so that they can learn more about Buddhism before they go back to their normal lives.

Where do monks live?

Monks live in a monastery. Sometimes they have their own room. Often they live in huts in the grounds of the monastery. The huts have very simple furniture – a small table or stool, and a mat to sleep on. In Zen Buddhism, all the monks may sleep in one big hall.

A monk does not own anything except the robes he wears, and necessary things like a bowl for food and a razor to shave his head. Anything else in the hut – for example, books or pens and paper – belong to the monastery, not the monk himself.

What do monks do?

Monks often spend most of the day on their own, reading and meditating. There is usually part of the day when they meet the other monks to read and meditate together. Many monks work as teachers or help people in some other way.

A Thai Buddhist monk studying outside his hut

All monks live very simple lives. They often eat only one meal a day, which is always before midday. After this they **fast** until the next day, though they are allowed to drink water.

Where do monks get their food?

Monks are given their food and everything they need by people who live near the monastery. Sometimes people give the monastery money instead. Giving the monks the things they need is called giving **alms**. It is not the same as begging, because people are pleased to give. Giving to the monks is part of a Buddhist's duty. It helps to earn merit for the person giving.

The five precepts

All Buddhists are expected to follow the five **precepts**, which are guides for living. They are:
- not to harm living things
- not to take what is not given
- to avoid improper sexual activity
- not to take part in improper speech
- to avoid alcohol and the misuse of drugs.

Buddhist monks and nuns also follow five other precepts. They agree not to:
- eat after midday
- attend music or dancing
- use perfume or jewellery
- sleep on a soft bed
- accept gifts of money.

Some other Buddhists follow these precepts, too.

New words

Alms giving food and necessities
Fast go without food and drink for religious reasons
Precept rule or guide for living

Test yourself

Where do monks live?

What is fasting?

What are alms?

What is a precept?

How many precepts do all Buddhists follow?

Think it through

1 What differences do you think you would notice between your school and living in a Buddhist monastery? Why do Buddhist boys go to school at the monastery?

2 Explain the difference between receiving alms and begging. Why do you think Buddhists are pleased to give to the monks?

3 Design a poster of the ten precepts which Buddhist monks and nuns follow. Explain them briefly in your own words.

Buddhism in Britain

This section tells you about Buddhism in Britain.

Until about a hundred years ago, Buddhism was almost unknown in Britain. Almost all Buddhists were in the countries where Buddhists had lived for hundreds of years. The first Buddhist missionary to teach in Britain arrived in 1893.

In the last hundred years, it has become more common for people to move to other countries to find work or a new life. Where Buddhists have done this they have taken their Buddhism with them. People are now more used to travelling to other countries, and learning about life there. Some people in Britain have become interested in the teachings of the Buddha, and have become Buddhists themselves.

Some people who have become Buddhists say that they like it because it does not ask them to believe anything they have not worked out for themselves. Others find that they agree with the teachings about the importance of taking care of everything in the world.

Buddhist monasteries in Britain

Most Buddhists in Britain do ordinary jobs. Most do not become monks or nuns, but there are some Buddhist monasteries. Monks and nuns live in the same way as they would where most people in the country are Buddhist. They live very simply, and meditate and teach.

Retreats

An important part of life in a Western monastery is arranging **retreats**. A retreat is a special time when people can leave their normal lives. They go to the monastery and

Inside a Buddhist temple in London

A Tibetan
Buddhist
monastery in
Scotland

live like a monk or nun for a few days or
weeks. This gives people the chance to be
with other Buddhists. They can also spend
more time meditating and reading the holy
books. They believe this makes them better
Buddhists in their normal lives.

Groups in Britain

In 1997, there were about 130,000
Buddhists living in Britain. The largest
number follow the teachings of Theravada
Buddhism. The next most popular is
Tibetan Buddhism, and then Zen
Buddhism. Some Buddhists are happy to
learn from all these groups.

Most groups have temples. Worship takes
place in the same way as it would in
countries where most people are Buddhist.
Group worship is usually on a Sunday, to fit
in with the British way of life.

New word

Retreats special times away from
   ordinary life

Test yourself

When did the first Buddhist missionary
   arrive in Britain?

What is a retreat?

About how many Buddhists live in
   Britain?

What school do most Buddhists in
   Britain follow?

Think it through

1 How many reasons can you think of
   why many people in Britain have
   become interested in Buddhism in
   the last hundred years?

2 How might a Buddhist explain why
   they want to go on retreat?

3 If possible, invite a Buddhist to come
   and talk to your group. If this is not
   possible, work in groups to find out
   as much as you can about
   Buddhism. Put together a short
   project called 'Buddhism in Britain'.

Special occasions I

This section tells you about important ceremonies for young Buddhists.

There are few teachings in Buddhism about birth and death, because for Buddhists they are only stages in the rebirth cycle. However, such events are very important, and most Buddhists follow their country's customs. This means that Buddhists in different countries may do things in quite different ways. This section looks at customs in Myanmar (Burma) and Thailand.

Birth

It is the custom for older relatives to prepare gifts for a new baby. A cradle is made ready, with clothes in it. When the baby is put in the cradle for the first time, the gifts are placed around it. The gifts are small useful things like books or tools which the child will need later in their life.

The head shaving ceremony

The main ceremonies for a baby happen when he or she is a month old. First, their head is shaved. The Buddha taught about life-forces which carry on from one life to the next. The hair is a symbol of a bad life-force from a previous life, so Buddhists want to get rid of it.

Then special cotton is tied around the baby's wrists, which the parents hope will bring it luck. The baby is often given its name at this ceremony. Sometimes monks are asked to suggest the name. Food is always given to the monks when a baby is born.

Joining a monastery

Many Buddhist boys join a monastery for a short time. This may be only for a few

A school for Buddhist monks in Thailand

**Many Buddhist boys
are taught by monks**

months. In Myanmar and Thailand, almost all boys join a monastery when they are about ten years old. This is so that they can be given an education by the monks.

The special ceremony when a boy joins the monastery is called **ordination**. In Myanmar, the boy acts out the story of Siddattha Gotama leaving his royal place and becoming a monk. There are special ceremonies and the boy's head is shaved.

(Almost all Buddhist monks have their heads shaved.) Older monks help him to dress in special monk's robes.

New word

Ordination ceremony in which a person becomes a monk or nun

Test yourself

Why is the baby's head shaved?

What is tied round the baby's wrist?

When is the baby given its name?

How old are boys when they join a monastery?

What is ordination?

Think it through

1 Why does Buddhism not have many teachings about birth and death?

2 What reasons can you think of why the baby's parents might ask a monk to suggest a name?

3 Write down as many words as you can which you think describe how you would feel if you were a Buddhist boy preparing for ordination. What do you think the most important feeling would be?

Special occasions II

This section tells you about the Buddhist ceremonies for marriage and death.

Marriage

In most Buddhist countries, the parents of a young man or woman suggest a person who would be suitable for them to marry. This is because marriage is so important. It joins two families.

When a couple have agreed to get married, astrologers suggest a good date for the wedding to take place. Astrologers are people who tell you about your future by studying the movement of the stars. Many people believe that this movement affects the sort of person you are and what happens in your life.

The marriage ceremony usually takes place in the bride's home. It is normally performed by a male relative of the bride, not by a monk. The couple stand on a platform called a **purowa**. They usually give each other rings, and the thumbs on their right hands are sometimes tied together. Their right wrists may be tied together with a silk scarf, instead. Children read special parts of the Buddhist holy books. The couple make promises that they will love and respect each other.

Sometimes a monk takes part in the wedding, and talks to the couple about the Buddha's teaching on marriage. If this does not happen at the wedding itself, the couple usually go to a monastery to listen to a talk there. At the end of the wedding, everyone shares a meal. The celebrations may go on for several days.

Death

The friends and relations of a person who has died are sad because someone they love is not with them any more. But Buddhists think that someone who has died will be reborn, so death is not the end. The funeral may be led by a monk who talks about the Buddha's teaching on what happens after death. Everyone repeats the Five Precepts and the Three Jewels. These are the most important Buddhist beliefs.

A Buddhist wedding in Malaysia